# Small

# Business 101

It doesn't have to be all that difficult.
It just needs to be done right!

# Table of Contents

*Chapter 1*

## The Basics of Small Business Ownership

If you ask others what the definition of a business is, you will get a variety of answers. They will all pretty much lead you to the same conclusion. I like Berg Bochner's definition of a **business**. He says, "A business is a legal entity structured to carry on a trade, service, or the production of goods. The entity has its own name, way of doing things, and some say even a personality."

There are basically four different types of business: a sole **proprietorship**, a **partnership**, a **corporation**, and the newest form - an LLC or **Limited Liability Corporation**. A sole proprietorship is just what it sounds like - a business that is owned and operated by an individual. A partnership is owned by two or more people having no shares. A corporation has shares or stocks. These stocks can be open to the public, or closed so that only family or friends can own them. Another thing to consider when developing a corporation is that they have double taxation. This means that shareholders are taxed on their income and the corporation is taxed at the corporate level. This is the only type of business that has the double taxation. There is a type of corporation called a s-corporation that only pays taxes once because the profits go to the owners and then they pay the tax. Then there is the new kid on the block, the LLC. It is a combination between a partnership and a corporation. There are still shareholders (otherwise known as stockholders), but they have a limited liability. This means that there cannot be anyone that lays claim against the individual owners of the company for losses.

There are different niches within the business world. A **retailer's** sole purpose is to sell something to the consumer. An example of a retail business would be Home Depot. The **supplier** (also known as the wholesaler or middleman) sells products to the retail business. An example of this would be MAB Paint here in Lafayette. A **producer** or manufacturer is the business who makes the goods and sells them to the suppliers. An example would be Dutch Boy Paint Company. The last type of business is the **service** business. This type is designed to help people or other businesses, but they do not sell a product. An example would be a painter.

How do you find your niche? Can anyone start a business? How old do you have to be? There are a lot more things involved in a business than just finding something you are good at or that you really enjoy, and selling/producing it. If you have a great idea, can your business survive? What if you are awesome at what you do? That is no guarantee! People start their own businesses for many reasons. Some of those reasons include financial success, wanting to be their own boss, to gain material wealth, to stay at home with family, or because they have something they believe will benefit others.

As you will learn in future lessons, there are a lot of things that go into the smallest business to the largest business. As Christians, our number one priority should be praying and seeking the Lord's will for our lives. If we have the go ahead, *then* we can proceed. Without that, keep seeking. It might not be the time for you, and only the Lord knows what the future holds! Every day of your life you need to continue turning your business over to God and allow Him to arrange the day.

A good business also takes good marketing, managers who understand the employees, an ability to sell the product or service, a passion about what you are selling or producing, a drive to succeed, good record keeping, and knowing the economic structure of the area. **Economics** is finding out the supply versus demand. To find out the supply and demand, do your homework  Find out if the business you are planning on starting is needed in your area, if the market is saturated, if people will pay for your product and how much, and who your target market is. The best way to discover if anyone is interested in purchasing your product or service is by talking to everyone you know, and even ones you don't know! A **target market** is the group of people who will be purchasing your product/service. Without knowing your target market and if your product is going to be sell able, you will not know who to market to, how much to produce/purchase, or what the selling price should be.

A lot of sole proprietors just fall into their business. They do not even know how the whole thing originated. Someone usually has a dream, but it is not always the owner. It is estimated that 85% of businesses in the United States are family owned! In the United States alone there are more than 1 million new businesses that start each year. Only 1/5 of them will survive. A business owner, who fails to plan, plans to fail! There are 6 things that you should have to get a business going:

1.  The dream to see it succeed
2.  The knowledge of your field
3.  Research in your field and market
4.  Training
5.  Personal interest
6.  The Lord's direction

Some people have the talent to see a need in their area and fill it. There are many different avenues that a business can take with our ever changing times and ready access to the Internet. There are several options businesses can offer, such as delivery services to your door, overnight shipping, and shop at home sales.

There are a few things to remember when planning on starting a new business concept in your area. Your idea will be copied by someone else, even with patents and trademarks! A **patent** is a document given by the United States of America to a business, that gives the business owner sole rights to an invention. A patent is usually good for 20 years. A **trademark** is anything distinguishing a company, such as a name, logo, phrase, symbol, or image. A trademark is generally good for the life of a business. It is not an easy process, and often help is needed from a lawyer. There are forms to fill out from the U.S. Patent and Trademark Office. This information is available on their website. Technology changes so quickly that you are not going to be able to stay on top of it and you will get competitors. Find something that makes you stand out from the rest.

You need to think of a creative business name. Check with the office of the Secretary of State to ensure that the name you will be using is available and not being used by someone else. You'll also need to a business license from the local tax office. All businesses must get a Federal Tax Identification Number from the IRS, and a business certificate from your county. A corporation or LLC will need to get incorporated in the state, and have on file the officers and directors (the people in charge). If selling a retail product, you will need to get a State Sales Tax permit. Some businesses require other specialized licenses or permits for environmental health and safety.

So what are **business ethics**? According to Webster's dictionary, this means the "study and examination of moral and social responsibility in relation to business practices and decision-making in business." As Christians, we have a God-given responsibility to respect our employees, our customers, our **vendors** (people we buy from), the people we work near, etc. As Christian business people, we need to strive for the highest levels at everything we do. We should have policies and procedures in place to help us with our ethics. It is a good idea to have these in writing and posted so that other employees can see what type of people we are and what we stand for.

Christians should stand out from the crowd. We should always deal fairly with everyone no matter what. We should not alter prices on every estimate just to get the deal. Keep the same working profit margin for each item that is being sold. Example: If selling carpet, wallpaper, and window treatments, there might be a 20% margin on carpet, 50% on window treatments, and 60% on wallpaper. Keep these mark-ups consistent for everyone. If you are dealing with large quantities then exceptions can be made, but do not change your standards to get a deal.

Also, as a Christian we need to consider why we have the business in the first place. Are you in it to make money? Are you filling a need in the community, such as no grocery stores within a 20 mile radius? What are your plans for the profit? Do you plan on using your profit for the Lord's work? Are you planning on buying all the toys you can imagine? It is very wise to take your profits and reinvest in your business, although make sure if you are making a profit that you are also tithing.

Also consider what type of filing system to use. You can use a computer, a notebook, envelopes, folders, a file cabinet with folders and labels, or just a ledger. Whatever you use, make sure to think about future expansion. You do not want to get so busy that you need to hire someone to work with you and hand them a notebook with papers hanging out and say, "Here are my files!" They might run out the door before they even begin! Have things as simple as this previously thought through.

There are some basic skills to use to promote yourself as a knowledgeable professional, even if you are young. First of all, be educated on the products! You also want to have good manners, both in person and on the telephone. It is okay to go tell the other person that you need to ponder their ideas or suggestions. You do not always have to give an answer right on the spot. Just get back with them in a timely manner.

Owners have many responsibilities, and one is to analyze if the business or different departments within it are growing too rapidly. When a business grows too quickly, there is a need to invest a substantial amount of money and time into the business. If the owner does not have liquid assets (cash), then they must fine another source for financing. This can be exceptionally difficult for a new business, as they do not have a lot of capital and often are already carrying debt and other loans.

Also, if the business begins doing large contracts, they generally do not pay as quickly as if it is a small sale. The reason for this is because large contracts pay in parts instead of the entirety at one time. Usually the scale is 25% down on signing of the contract and partial payments throughout. Then, when the job is finished and the business is satisfied, they pay the balance that is left.

Another reason a business could fail because of growing too large too fast is in the essence of time. For example, a service cleaning business which takes on too many contracts at one time but does not have the manpower to fill these positions could burn themselves out or not perform the service to the best of their abilities, resulting in loss of contracts.

Some other things to look at in analyzing a business would be:
1. Moving to a new/larger location can cause a decrease in business

2. Taking on too much debt/rent, sales cannot always compensate properly

3. Poor customer service is a reason for customers not to return

4. Purchasing too much of certain products is a problem because they may not sell quick enough or the profit margin is too small, which leads to poor cash flow

5. Not having enough training or knowledge on the products that are being sold is a reason for consumers not to return, and instead seek that knowledge from competing stores.

6. Purchasing items impulsively rather than seeing the real reason you would like to purchase an item can result in loss of profit.
   a. An example would be a business that does not understand their consumers - therefore items are purchased which are not relevant to the consumers.
   b. Another example would be purchasing office equipment that far out seeds what the business needs or can afford.

7. If a firm is doing well, the owners taking too much money out and not re-investing the profits can lead to trouble.   The business can fall fast without anyone noticing until it is too late.

8. If a business does not take the time to thank its customers it could easily lose 20% of its clients before they even begin to realize what is happening.  It takes time to build more clients to replace former ones.

*Questions To Keep You Thinking*

1. Are a husband and wife a sole proprietorship or a partnership?

2. Do partnerships have to be split equally? Give your opinion.

3. Can you be a producer and a retailer? Give an example.

4. Can you be a producer, retailer, and a supplier? Give an example.

5. In your opinion, how many hours a week do you think a person starting up a business should put in every week?

6. Give 2 examples each of both professional and unprofessional telephone skills.

7. List 10 trademarks that you can think of.

8. What are the four types of businesses? Describe them.

*What Category Does This Business Fit In?*

Draw a line to match up what category goes with what business.

a. Builder                                    Wholesale

b. Production Line                    Construction

c. Mining                                  Manufacturing

d. Performer                                    Service

e. Cellular Service                    Raw Materials

f. Costco/Sam's Club        Telecommunications

*Chapter 2*

## Writing a Business Plan

A **business plan** is like a road map for a business. This is where you plan to see your business in one year, three years, five years, ten years, and so on. You'll continue referring back to it, to make sure you are on the right track. It is easy to get wound up in day to day operations of a business and lose track of where you are heading. Writing a business plan is no small task! Most people put 50 – 100 hours into writing one, and take about 6 months research it.

Growing up, my dad started a lot of different businesses - this kind of person is called an **entrepreneur**. He started retail operations, wholesale, and manufacturing businesses. He was not one to be very organized. My mom did most of the book work and organizing of the businesses. Dad considered his ministry to be helping other business people start their business and run them ethically. He counseled people weekly in keeping a Christian focus on their business. He mainly had sole proprietorships, although he did have one partnership. I saw him write many contracts on napkins and table mats in restaurants. I also saw him shake hands to close a deal. One thing I never saw him do was write a business plan. He has been unable to remain in business because he has Alzheimer's, and the last business he started closed last year. I believe it was partly due to the fact no one knew where he wanted the business to go, what goals he wanted to reach, and what dreams he had. This is just one example of why it is important to write a business plan.

An important part of your business plan is the **mission statement**. This will briefly describe what your values, goals, and plan for your business will be. It is important to keep this visible, both for the public to see and also for the employees. It is a good reminder of why you are in business and what you aspire to accomplish. As a Christian business person, your ethics can be what sets you apart. Employees need to know what you stand for and how you want your business run. Some mission statements are quite lengthy, although I recommend keeping it under three sentences. It is helpful to memorize it so that it is always on your mind.

A business plan needs to start by addressing some basic issues. Those can include:
1. When you are actually starting your business
2. Where it will begin
3. What the name is going to be
4. What type of structure it will have

5. How many employees you have and what their jobs are
6. Policies for your employees
7. What type of investment needs you have
8. What your short term and long term goals are
9. Who is your target market
10. What kind of spending habits does your target market have
11. What is the perfect customer
12. Who is your competition
13. What your competition offers in their marketing
14. What is your marketing strategy
15. How you are going to set up your bookkeeping
16. When you anticipate breaking even (financial breakeven point)
17. What your profit and loss forecast is.

When your business is going to open can be an easy question, although if you do not take in all of the factors you might not be on schedule. Things to remember include ordering signage, having all of your merchandise labeled and stocked, having advertisements ready to go, and having your computers and point of sale programs up and running.

Where your business will begin is a pretty simple question to answer. If you plan on expanding, you will want to write down the location you are considering and when you are considering the expansion. It is good to begin thinking about this, even if it's not expected for 10 years. Write it down, it will be helpful later.

You will probably go through a plethora of names before you come up with one that you settle on. Ask others to help you come up with a business name. Think about the colors and details to be used in the logo. It can become expensive to make forms and business cards if there are a lot of colors or details.

Do you want to open a sole proprietorship, partnership, corporation, or a LLC? Is your business one that might have a lot of liability? Do you have excessive amounts of assets to protect? Are you willing to spend more money to become something other than a sole proprietorship?

How many employees do you need to be able to open? Can you do it by yourself? How many employees do you anticipate needing in 1 year, 3 years, and so on? What types of jobs will employees have? Don't forget to think about things like cleaning the kitchen and bathrooms - will you do this or have it hired out? Who will do your bookkeeping? Will you need a lawyer, and if so, who? Will you be offering any kinds of insurance, benefit packages, vacation to the employees? Determine the pay scale and how to reach those levels, and what percentages to give for raises. Have an employee handbook designed especially for your business.

Do you have the capital it will take to start your business? If you need to seek a loan, who will it be from, when will you pay it back, and at what interest rates will that be attainable? Remember, you will not immediately have customers pouring in - you will need to first invest a lot of money in order to draw people into the business.

What goals are there for your business in one year, three years, five years, and 25 years? What will you do if you need assistance? Will a family member step in or would you close or sell the business? What would you like your sales to be in each year? Would you like to be selling on the

Internet?  Would you like to bring in new product lines at certain intervals?

Think about what makes you unique - a term for this is **Unique Selling Position** (USP).  The lowest price does not guarantee that people are going to buy from you.  A high price with great service and quality often results in high sales.  Maybe you operate the cleanest gas station in town...here has to be something unique about your business! It can be price, quality, convenience of shopping, the service you offer, or a strong guarantee.  Maybe you have a product that is the same as other people, but you plan on marketing it differently.  You could **out promote** (which means to push a specific product more than other businesses are), out advertise, or outspend your competition.

As one can see, it takes a lot of homework to research a possible business!  It is not easy to get to know the competition, but it is very useful.  Discovering who your competition is can be as easy as looking through the newspapers or phone books, and listening to the radio, along with visiting their locations.  Pay particular attention to what is attracting people to the competition's location. Is it the sales they offer?  The cleanliness, customer service, employee knowledge of products, their selection, or are they the only store like it in town?

After looking at the competition, pay attention to their advertising jingles; start thinking of how you would like to be set apart.  What kind of plans can you come up with that would be advertising with a twist?  Don't try to mimic theirs - come up with fresh and unique ways of advertising.

How are you going to set up your bookkeeping? Are you going to use a computer program or an accountant to do your accounting? Will you be hiring someone to help you with this or are you going to do this yourself? If you are doing it yourself, what kind of knowledge or background is needed? There are agencies out there that help set up bookkeeping software and teach you how to use the program.

Your **breakeven point** is when you are making money. All of the initial debt is paid off that was invested into the business. A business needs to figure out if it is making money, on what products, and what percentage it is making. This is partially done by finding out what the breakeven point is, and you can do this for individual products or for the business as a whole. An example of finding the breakeven point for a product would be if a retail location purchased items to sell, has sold them, and has now has begun making a profit off of these items (instead of investing other funds toward this purchase).
The calculation for this is Fixed Costs / Unit Price = Break Even Point.
Unless every item has been broken down, it is easier to look at a business' "whole picture." Do this by looking at the amount of money that has been invested initially, and when all of the debt was paid off. If the business is functioning entirely on its own (including covering monthly expenses), it is at the breakeven point.

A **profit and loss analysis forecast** is what the business is perceived be making in certain time increments. Doing a forecast like this will help set goals for sales and production. This forecast is prepared by estimating what anticipated expenses will be and what anticipated sales will be, and compiling this information. This then gives employees sales projections that are attainable to strive for, and gives the owner a goal for the business. This forecast may be revised each month, each quarter, or each year. For a small business, I recommend yearly. It is fun to look at what the business forecasts were when the firm was originally opened, and how the profit and loss analysis has changed over a period of years!

*Questions To Keep You Thinking*

1. How necessary do you think it is to have a business plan?

2. Do you feel it is important to have all of the parts listed above in every business plan? Why?

3. How often do you think you need to read your business plan?

4. How often do you think you should revise your business plan?

### Chapter 3

## Forms, Contracts and Pricing

A **contract** is an agreement between two or more parties to perform a service for the other party in exchange for goods or services. A contract even among friends is always a good idea. A contract is not to show that you do not trust another person, instead, it is to avoid verbal miscommunication and misunderstandings. Many times it is a good idea to have a lawyer draw up a contract, especially if it is a partnership.

There are different types of contracts, all honored to some manner by the court system. There are **written contracts**, which are binding agreements. And there are **verbal contracts**, which are generally acknowledged with a handshake. Verbal contracts can sometimes have disputes. Verbal contracts are somewhat binding, but it is still your word against someone else's.

All contracts should have in them the names of all the parties involved, date the contract was written and signed, duties to be performed by both parties, what amount of money is to be paid or received, dates to have the work completed by and payment received by, and signatures of all parties involved. It is highly recommended to read a contract before signing it to ensure that nothing other than what had been specified is in the contract, and that no typo's have been made (especially in the dollar category).

Do not feel like you need to accept the first contract. You can negotiate to get what is fair to all involved. Listen and learn what the other party wants and throw in a free service or a referral if that will help to make the deal. Do not let someone get you to cut your prices just because you are young and they feel you don't know how to handle a business. This does happen.

If you later need to change part of the contract, an addendum will need to be added. An **addendum** is a change made to a contract, added to the end, signed, and dated. This will change only part of the contract, and it is not required to write a whole new contract. The addendum will serve as the new contract for the specific area revised.

An **appraisal** is a document showing the value of something. Generally, this is used in taxes, real estate, or insurance. When inquiring about insurance, get an appraisal from several different agencies.

If you were going to be building a new building and wanted contractors to look at the building plans and tell you how much they would charge you to do that job, they would give you an estimate. An **estimate** is a document showing how much something will cost and how long it will take to complete. This is the difference between an appraisal and an estimate. How does an estimate differ from a contract? An estimate is just that - it is not binding because no work has been agreed to be done. If there is an acceptance of an estimate, then it will become a contract. Sometimes it will be in writing and sometimes it will only be verbal.

A bid is often used as a slang term by contractors when they are talking about an estimate. A definition of a **bid** is actually a formal agreement to purchase something at a specified price, such as at an auction.

Sometimes business people exchange product for product - this is called **barter** or **trade**. When one company has something that another company desires, they might offer to exchange a product for a product. There are companies called Barter Corporations or Trade Exchanges that you can become a member of. Members of these organizations can purchase from anyone within this organization rather than just one business. Each business has an account, and any transaction that is bought or sold is put into an account for your business. Instead of a checking account, you have a barter account, enabling you to spend your barter dollars on companies within the organization.

The wallpaper business I was in was involved with three Barter Corporations. We would sell vertical blinds at 50% trade/50% cash, wallpaper at 100% trade/0% cash, and carpet at 0% trade/100% cash. This gave us the ability to sell to consumers we never would have reached if we were not members of these organizations. Every type of product you sell is categorized with how much cash and how many trade dollars. One year, we purchased a swimming pool, and it was paid for with our barter dollars.

> Example: A wallpaper company has 12,000 barter dollars; a pool costs $9,000; the pool company will accept 100% trade/no cash. The wallpaper company purchases the pool for $9000, dropping their barter dollars to 3,000 barter dollars and increasing the pool company to 9,000 more barter dollars.

When writing up any type of proposal, make sure to get all the details of what the customer wants, the name and address of the customer for billing, the physical address that you will be doing the work at, and who will pay for what items (such as insurance and equipment rental). Be sure to break everything down in detail, have solutions to potential problems, and have written in exactly what will be included and covered. Highlight and verbally clarify the final cost!

A **breach of contract** is when one party does the work that had been agreed upon, and the other party does not follow his/her part of the contract involving payment or exchange of goods and services. If this happen, there are several ways to getting this resolved; the first and most admirable way would be to talk calmly and politely to the other party. The second is to send a polite letter – and keep a copy for your records along with the date and by whom the letter was received by. The last and least favorable way is to go to court. This is a very expensive and long process. For a small business, this could eat up all of the assets pretty quickly. Weigh if it is worth it to go through all of the expense.

When working with other Christians, please do not think that you do not need to make a contract. I have dealt with many "Christian" business people who do not follow through on what has been agreed upon by both parties. This is not to say that all Christian business people would not follow through on contracts. The Bible reminds us in Romans 3:22 – 24

> *"This righteousness from God comes through faith in Jesus Christ to all who believe. There is no difference, 23 for all have sinned and fall short of the glory of God, 24 and are justified freely by his grace through the redemption that came by Christ Jesus."*

We are not to judge whom is saved or unsaved. As Christians, we are to practice smart thinking - and that means in business as well. We do need to rely on the gut instincts given to us by the Holy Spirit to show us what moves to take.

Please consider all of your practices and let your Yes be Yes and your No be No. If you have said you are going to do something, as a Christian it is binding.

James 5:12 states, "Above all, my brothers, do not swear— not by heaven or by earth or by anything else. Let your 'Yes' be yes, and your 'No', no, or you will be condemned." This can be as small as telling your parents you will take out the garbage! You better do it!

The first contract in the Bible was between Laban and Jacob. Jacob wanted to marry Laban's daughter, Rachel. In exchange, Laban said "work for me for 7 years and she will be yours." The problem was that Laban had an older daughter, Leah, who was not yet married - and it was the custom for the older to be married first. After Jacob worked the 7 years, Laban did not follow through on his agreement with Jacob. He gave Jacob Leah instead. Laban and Jacob then made another agreement, and Jacob worked another 7 years in order to marry Rachel. He then worked even longer for cattle, taking only the least productive for himself (although the Lord made his the most productive). Read the whole story in Genesis 29 and 30!

An example of a mutual contract being dissolved is found in Exodus 4:18. In Exodus 2, Moses had fled to Midian and helped a priest named Jethro who had seven daughters. The girls always went to a well to water their cattle, and Moses helped them get it done quickly. Exodus 2:21 speaks of an agreement between Moses and Jethro in which Moses would stay and work for Jethro if Jethro agreed to give Moses his daughter Zipporah's hand in marriage. In the meantime, Moses had become an outcast in his own country (remember that the Israelites were slaves to Egypt during this time). The Lord showed himself to Moses in the burning bush and told him to go to Pharaoh in Egypt and ask for God's people to be let go. In order to do this, Moses needed to ask Jethro if he could go, since his leaving would mean that he would not be able to fulfill his part of the contract. Jethro saw that Moses was doing as God had commanded him, and said for him to go, and take his family, too. So, this contract was dissolved by mutual consent.

The most powerful contract ever dissolved involved Christ's dying on the cross. In Colossians 2:13-15, we read:
> "13 When you were dead in your sins and in the uncircumcision of your sinful nature, God made you alive

*with Christ. He forgave us all our sins, 14 having canceled the written code, with its regulations, that was against us and that stood opposed to us; he took it away, nailing it to the cross. 15 And having disarmed the powers and authorities, he made a public spectacle of them, triumphing over them by the cross."*

What a great "deal" we received when that contract was dissolved!

Some words you might hear tossed around are **gross profit** and **gross profit margin**. These words have different meanings. Here are the formulas.

Total Net Sales – Total Cost of Sales = Gross Profit

Gross Profits / Total Net Sales = Gross Profit Margin.

A good thing to think about is how to determine price, whether it be for a service or on individual products. For a service business, there are different types of billing. An **hourly billing rate** is where you bill out per hour worked, generally in 15 minute increments. **Flat rate billing** (also called standard rate) is when you do the same type of service for all different types of people - you will choose to bill a flat rate. The third way is called a **retainer** or a fee charged monthly. This is kind of like a monthly deposit made to keep someone available whenever you need them. Generally, this is charged by lawyers. If you have a retail business and have products to sell, determine the mark-up. First, determine what the expenses or overhead is going to be, then work up from there. If you have a storefront, you will need to calculate in those costs. If your business deals with sub-contractors, you will need to consider that cost in your pricing. As a general rule, mark the price they charge up 15 – 20% - this will cover insurances, equipment rentals, etc. Generally, you cannot work on less than a 35% profit margin. However, all products will not be the same profit margin. There are some companies who operate on virtually no profit margin on some products or services, in order to get rid of the competition. As a Christian, this is an unfair and unethical business practice. Hey, competition is not always a bad thing! It keeps you on your toes and stimulates creativity.

When considering profit margin and pricing, think about what type of store you are. There are three general types: **high-end** such as a boutique, **middle-end** such as a retail operation, and **low-end** such as a discount store. Know what competition is in each of those types and what the suggested mark-up for your products are from the manufacturer. If you are the manufacturer, check the mark-up pricing in that industry. That information can be researched in trade magazines and journals or by purchasing the information. Some sources for that are;
- http://www.hoovers.com
- http://www.plunkettresearch.com

In figuring **overhead** (what basic monthly expenses are going to cost), consider things such as rent, utilities, insurance, and property taxes. These expenses do not change very much - in fact, utilities can be put on a **fixed payment plan** where the rate is the same every month for the whole year. When calculating overhead, there are **variable monthly expenses** to consider as well as your fixed expenses; these would include things such as shipping and handling, merchandise being purchased, and services.

Other common terms that are used are **gross** or **net**. These terms are used along with many things such as salary and profit to name a few. Gross is the total. Net is the gross minus the costs and expenses. So, if you receive $20.00 per hour salary – that is your gross salary. Once taxes are taken out, it becomes your net salary.

There is a standard way to figure out what pricing needs to be for a service business. The way to do this is:

Take the Yearly Salary you desire;
- **Plus** the Overhead (fixed costs)
- **Plus** the Annual Profit you desire (~20%)
- **Divided by** the Annual Billable Hours
- **Equals** the Hourly Rate

So let's break that down using these figures. You start with what you think you are worth (your desired salary). In this example, let's say $50,000 per year (annually). Add your annual overhead, $20,000 and then add your 20% profit of $14,000. Finally, divide by the total billable hours annually of 1000 (50 weeks x 20 hours per week = 1000). This will equal an hourly rate of $84.00 per hour.

There is a wealth of knowledge needed in starting a business! One area I recommend you seek help in is insurance. You will need liability insurance, property insurance, auto insurance, workers compensation, health insurance, business interruption insurance (when business has to be stopped due to a catastrophe). For a small home based business, an agent can look under the terms listed for your home insurance, and it might be covered for sales up to $10,000.00 annually.

**Liability insurance** is insurance for what the policyholder is legally obligated to pay because of bodily injury or property damage caused to another person. For example, if someone fell at your place of employment, this insurance would cover the cost of their medical bills. **Worker's Compensation** protects workers when they are disabled or injured at the workplace. This will protect them by giving them monetary support while they are out of work. There is a limit to how much is dispersed. **Health insurance** is a policy that will pay specified sums for medical expenses or treatments. Health policies can offer many options and vary in the coverage. For a small business, health insurance is a very large expense. Many small business owners have high deductibles, or they might have spouses who work at large organizations that can carry the family's health plans. Most small business owners cannot afford dental or eye coverage. If you have automobiles owned by the business you will need to have **auto insurance** for them. This works pretty much the same way as an individual's auto policy. There is generally a discount if there are more than two vehicles on a plan. **Property insurance** is just that - the protection of the property against fire, theft, or other uncontrollable circumstances. It will cover the contents as well, so if you start with a small inventory and then expand, or add an expensive piece of equipment, let your insurance agent know so that adjustments can be made.

I have read that there is an organization called the American Small Business Association (ASBA). From my understanding, it is mainly to help small businesses have access to the same things that bigger corporations do (such as affordable health insurance). They have a yearly membership fee, and you receive a newsletter, and courses on business planning, writing a business plan, business discounts, and finding affordable medical insurance. I have never used this, but it might be worth looking into. Health insurance is extremely expensive!

*Questions To Think You Thinking*

1. What would be an example of a good or service exchanged for in a contract? What is it called?

2. Give an example of each of the following: bid, appraisal, estimate, and a contract.

Chapter 4

# Accounting Basics

Accounting is a very difficult class to understand unless you dig in and find out how everything works. It is crucial to know some important things about accounting. With most of my businesses we had accountants set up accounting software to maintain our books. Being brief on accounting is difficult for me so most of my information was from reading and researching many books and web sites, with the two favorites being <u>Bookkeeping Made Simple</u> by David A. Flannery and http://www.accountingcoach.com.

There are many different accounting software programs. Some you might be familiar with, such as Peachtree, QuickBooks, MYOB, and Microsoft Office Small Business

Accounting. I won't go into all of the software available, because it is more important to know basic accounting before starting on a software program. This, like the other chapters you've read so far, is just a small glimpse into what happens in accounting in hopes of familiarizing you with some terms, and the appearance of several different reports and journals.

The most important thing in accounting is to make sure you are organized. Without organization the books will be very difficult to keep and things quickly become chaos. Make sure you have a good file system from the beginning; this can evolve with time depending on your needs as you grow.

Next, make sure your original entries are in the proper place! I would highly recommend hiring a professional to set up your initial bookkeeping records. When using an accountant every month, all that is needed is to give him or her a copy of a software file backup that includes the totals for the month. The accountant makes sure all of the entries are in their proper spots. If a firm desires to do it themselves without an accountant, and chooses to use a manual method, it can be a relatively easy process if the right knowledge has been acquired. If your business is very small, you can even use an Excel Spreadsheet to do your charting. Whatever a business chooses, they need to make sure to keep all of the receipts, and keep everything organized in a way that anyone can decipher it.

We will talk about some basic terms and equations (well, *accountants* consider them "basic!").

A **transaction** is anything involving the shifting of money from one location to another. An **account** is where the money or entries are transferred and recorded. There are different **reports** that you will use; some of them more frequently than others. They include: Profit & Loss Statement, Income & Expense Report, Accounts Payable (A/P), Accounts Receivable (A/R), Balance Sheet, Cash Flow, Budget, Journal and several others.

**Assets** are anything that is owned, whether you have it completely paid for or not. An example would be a building you have put a down payment on, but do not own in full. Other examples would be inventory, materials, equipment owned, cash on hand, and land. There are two kinds of assets. **Current assets** are constantly changing, such as inventory, supplies, and accounts receivable that turn into cash. The other kinds of assets are **Capital assets** - these are things like the land, buildings, and equipment. Capital asset items depreciate over time.

**Equity** is any kind of debt that a business owes. There are two types of equity; owner's and liabilities. **Owner's equity** is the amount remaining after taking the assets minus the liabilities. Sometimes we call this capital, or net worth. **Liabilities** can include money owed to suppliers or vendors, taxes, any type of loans - anything the business owes to someone else. Liabilities also have two categories: long-term and current. The difference is that current is to be repaid within one year, long-term is anything longer than one year. The fixed expenses or long-term liabilities are items you continue owing on whether you are in business or not such as: automobiles payments and insurance; they must have a useful life of more than one year, such as computers or desks. A portion of these fixed expenses are deducted each year for the anticipated life span of the item this is called **depreciation**. Current liabilities are things that have a useful life of less than one year, and they are not depreciated.

The most basic accounting equation is that all assets must equal liabilities + equities (A = L + E). The following example was taken from Bookkeeping Made Simple.

> You purchase a car for $25,000 and the dealer gave you $5,000 in trade for your old car and you borrow $20,000 from the bank. You would have a $25,000 car and owe $20,000 to the bank. To the bookkeeper, you would have: $25,000 (A) = $20,000 (L) + $5,000 (E).

When beginning a business, decide if you will be doing cash basis accounting or accrual basis accounting. When you count your income as you receive it and your expenses when you write the checks, this is called **cash basis accounting**. **Accrual basis accounting** is when sales are made and billed out you count as income, and when you receive bills you put that in your records as having paid out. The problem is that you are not really sure what the cash flow actually is with the accrual basis accounting. But, if you stock inventory and have a retail location, the government requires the use of the accrual method of accounting.

**Revenue** is any money the business earns. A company can earn **sales revenue**, which is money earned from the sale of a product. **Service revenue** is money earned from a service performed. **Net Income** is a term used to describe what is left after everything is subtracted from revenue. The formula for this is:

Revenue – Expenses = Net Income

Revenue and expenses are broken down on the Income Statement to show what the firm's net income is.

A **journal** or **general journal** is a place where you will record transactions chronologically. A t-account is a ledger with an account name having 2 columns - a debit and a credit column. The debit (DR) column is always on the left and the credit (CR) column is always on the right. There are some rules for debits and credits.

1. Assets increase with Debits and decrease with Credits.
2. Expenses increase with Debits and decrease with Credits.
3. Liabilities increase with Credits and decrease with Debits.
4. Owner's Equity increases with Credits and decreases with Debits.
5. Revenue increase with Credits and decrease with Debits.

The key is to see what type of entry you will be making, and then you will know if it will increase or decrease the accounts in the postings. **Posting** a transaction means transferring the information from the journal into the accounts. Every time a bookkeeper enters a transaction into a journal, they must think through the following process:

1. What accounts are affected by this entry? If more than one entry is affected, it's called a **compound entry**.
2. Are these accounts assets, liabilities, revenues, expenses, or owner's equity?
3. Does the transaction increase or decrease them, using the questions above?

4. Does this information call for a debit entry or credit entry using the questions above?

A **ledger** has a page for each customer, the cash account, every expense account, etc. On the very first page is a **chart of accounts**, which is a list of all of the accounts and the numbers that are assigned to them. A **worksheet** is where any adjustments are made to prepare for the financial statements. **Financial statements** are the balance sheets and income statements - they are prepared from the worksheets.

When an item that is posted on a journal line is written into the account ledger, put the line number from the journal in the account ledger. It's also important to write in the account number from the journal. All of this duplication is called **cross-referencing**. If there is an error, this will help locate where the error has been made. In accounting, it is very important to check and double check everything while you are doing it, because it is hard to trace mistakes later. If you have trouble balancing, here are some things to look for:

- If you are off by 9 or any number divisible by 9, there is a **transposition error**. This means a number has been written in backwards.
- If you have written a decimal in the wrong place it is called a **slide error**. The number will be off by 10, 100, 1,000, etc.
- If the number is evenly divided by 2, it is probably a duplicate debit or credit posting, or a debit posted as a credit, or vice versa.
- Check the adding again to make sure it is correct.
- Look for a number in the debit and credit column that matches the number that you are off.

A **trial balance** sheet is created at the end of each month. It is where the accounts are totaled and balanced. To design a trial balance sheet, a business needs to:

1. Categorize accounts and place their totals in the correct debit or credit columns
2. Total all of the debit and credit ledger columns
3. Subtract total smaller number from the larger number
4. Place the remaining number called the **balance** in the larger amount column

If a business did not take a regular inventory of an item such as copier paper or envelopes, the trial balance sheet would need adjusted for that. Depreciation also gets adjusted on the **adjusted trial balance sheet**. This is a very important worksheet, and it can have up to 10 columns. Five of the columns are debits and 5 are credits. The five categories include:

- Unadjusted Trial Balance – columns 1 & 2
- Adjustments – columns 3 & 4
- Adjusted Trial Balance – columns 5 & 6
- Income statement – columns 7&8 (optional)
- Balance Sheet – columns 9&10

An **income statement** is a quick glimpse into how a business is doing. It is also called a **Profit and Loss Statement**. This is a list of all the income over a period of time such as one week, one month, or one year. The information for the income statement comes from columns 7 and 8 of the worksheet. The last line of this report shows the business's net income or bottom line.

The **balance sheet** is prepared from columns 9 and 10 of the worksheet. This shows everything a business owned (assets), everything owed (liabilities), and what is left (owner's equity). *The balance sheet must always balance!*

Assets are on the left column and liabilities are on the right column (it is set up differently than a ledger). On this form, the current assets and liabilities are broken down from the capital assets and long-term liabilities.

Assets – Liabilities = Owner's Equity

The last step is **closing the books** - this is used to prepare for the next fiscal year. To close the books, it is necessary to bring all of the revenue and expense accounts to zero. There are three steps to this:
1. Bringing all revenue accounts to zero
    a. Debit every revenue account
    b. Credit the income summary account with a total of all revenues
2. Bringing all expense accounts to zero
    a. Credit each expense account
    b. Debit the income summary account with a total of all expenses
3. Balancing the Income Summary and Adjusting Owner's Equity Account. Add the Debit and Credit columns in the income summary account getting a total.
    a. If the firm has made a profit you will have a Credit, then you will debit the income summary account and credit the Owner's Equity account.
    b. If the firm has had a loss, you will have a Debit, then you will credit the Income Summary Account and debit the Owner's Equity Account.

*Chapter 5*

## Advertising & Marketing

There are many different definitions on advertising and marketing. Some people think they are the same thing, others say they are completely different. We are going to go with the following definitions as we talk about these terms. **Advertising** is announcing your business in the media's view via billboards, radio, television, and newspapers. Basically, advertising is attracting people so that they buy from you. **Marketing** is the all-encompassing day to day business of buying, selling, displaying, shipping and storing products for your business. An easy way to remember marketing is how you sell your product or service.

Now that we know what advertising is, how do we find out who to advertise to? The focus should be on our **target market**, the group or type of people who will use your goods and services. Knowing this market helps increase sales, and they can be used to try out new products and services. If you do not get your name out to the right people, you won't sell your product or service! For example, if you advertise on the local oldies radio station that has an audience of middle aged men, and you are trying to sell skateboards, you are not going to sell very many! But, if you hand out fliers at the batting cages or put a jingle on the pop rock station, you are apt to sell more skateboards. The best way to find your target market is to ask other people. Remember, before you started your business you needed to ask different people if they would be interested in your products and services? This is how to find your niche - ask questions to a variety of people and take surveys

There are so many different avenues of advertising. Here are just a few: radio and television, newspapers and magazines, direct mail pieces, Internet, telephone poles, place mats, going door–to–door, billboards, networking groups, or handing out fliers and business cards. The most important type of advertising that showcases your business is word of mouth advertising!

When you launch a new retail business, some places offer a special **promotion**. Some examples of promotions are any type of give-a-way, clowns, "2 for the price of 1" sales, limited time only sales, "buy one get one half off" sales, and profits for charity sales. Businesses usually either offer these special promotions frequently for certain groups of people, or have them several times a year for the general public. Consumers love sales! Whether it is 10% off or 90%

off, consumers look for what they think is a bargain. A great example of this is Kohl's. They always have something on sale, and if you just wait a week or two whatever you want will be on sale. When you spend money on promotional material, make sure it has your business name, logo, phone number, and address.

For a business logo, you can use the business name and put it in a fancy script, or you could use your picture or another image to show who you are. Logos can be as simple or as complex as you would like them to be. Make sure the logo is on everything! If you are creating a complex logo, think about what types of promotional materials it will be used on to see if it will be cost effective to print it. The more complex and the more colors used, the higher the price of printing. Also, when developing promotional materials for a business, it is a good idea to have quotes of praise (testimonials) from other consumers. Even a few go a long ways. Consumers are often more fearful of purchasing from a new business if it does not have any positive references.

A relatively new way to get into the business industry and meet a lot of professionals is through networking groups. In every city there are plenty to choose from. Here in Lafayette, there is *Lafayette Business to Business*, *Lafayette Champions*, and *Rainmakers* to name a few. Generally, the newspaper will have the names of different groups and when they meet. There are groups that have the same name throughout the world and keep the same policies. Each of them will be slightly different depending on the local group leaders and members. It is best to check out several different groups before settling on one. As a general rule, you are only to be involved in one networking group at a time. Some of the networking groups require that you generate leads for other members. What this means is that you are required to bring other business professionals names of consumers who could use their services. This is a great way to generate a lot of leads. Other groups are more family oriented - where everyone gets to know each other and strives to build business through relationships. When involved in a networking group, it is proper to offer lower prices or services to the business professionals in the group. Always have a business card handy. It has been said that the average person will only wait 4 seconds for a business card!

Let's move on to the aspect of marketing your business. As mentioned earlier, this is the all-encompassing area of sales, product development, merchandising, promotion, distribution, service, and sales and pricing. There are 7 key components that we are going to be looking at.

1. **Product development and service**. Evaluate what your profit margin (percentage of profit vs. overall total sales) is going to be. How easy is it to sell and produce your product? Know who you are targeting - this is the only way to know if you will be spending advertising money wisely. With competition (and if you don't have any yet, be prepared because it is coming!), what are you going to offer that is different than theirs; a better price, a better quality, more service?

2. **Advertising**. What types of advertising will be cost effective? How will you inform customers that you are open for business, and what's the best way to influence them to purchase your products or services? Whether you have a retail location or not, people aren't going to just start swarming in! You have to *draw* customers in. Be creative and unique, but also stick to the point and keep it simple. Design jingles and catchy phrases that

will stick with people, and keep them consistent in all of your advertising. Make sure to have the finances to implement your ideas. Even the yellow page ads are very expensive, but it is important to have your name in them so that people know how to find you.

There is a great advantage in having computers help design your advertising. When thinking of designs for logos, business cards, web sites and promotional materials, remember to play around with the fonts, size, and colors. Some key colors are:

- Black – Power, Authority, Elegance
- Brown – Stability, Masculine, Natural
- Dark Blue – Power, Knowledge, Integrity, Strength
- Light Blue – Softness, Energetic, Tranquil
- Purple – Nobility, Luxury
- Green – Healing, Restful, Growing
- Red – Leadership, Courage, Boldness
- White – Purity, Cleanliness, Goodness
- Yellow – Energetic, Joyful, Fun, Happiness

Consider these colors and their meanings when designing advertising. Small changes in color, font, and size can impact marketing. Color is very important in attracting attention to whatever medium of advertising that is chosen. Another important thing to consider is the font style that will be used - keep it crisp, clean and easy to read. Keep all of your advertising materials simple, an extension of you and your business, and keep it short and to the point. Do not ramble on about all of the products and services available. Advertising is just to get people's attention, and then once you have their attention they will want to know more. It is so important to keep your name out there. It takes, on average, 14 exposures to a product before a consumer will purchase it!

3. **Networking**. We discussed this briefly in our section on advertising. There are other ways to network which I did not mention previously. They include the Chamber of Commerce, Rotary Clubs, church, friends, your children's friends, relatives, and specialized groups such as women business owners. The newspaper or other business people are the best ways to find out what available for networking. Most new businesses cannot afford to join all sorts of organizations, so check out several before joining one. You can also start your own if you do not have many in town, or if they do not fill your needs. If you have children or siblings, go to their baseball games, and try to sponsor some of those events. Let others know what you do! Build relationships first - do not always try to sell yourself or your product. Building relationships with your friends, colleagues, and clients is crucial in developing a good business.

4. **Publicity**. This can be free advertising! Call local newspapers and magazines and ask them to write an article about your business. Give talks to networking groups or college classes, telling about your services and business specialty. Each of us have a wealth of information within us! Use this to write articles or give talks - these do not have to be only about your business. Just give a brief mention that you own a business, the name, location, and what you sell. This will be one more place where the public has heard the business name. I cannot say enough how important it is to keep that name in front of people.

5.  **Distribution**. How you are going to get your product or service into the hands of the consumer? There are **indirect sales** and **direct sales**. Indirect sales use sales people to sell to small and large size companies. This can include having hired sales people, or doing all of the sales yourself. An example would be designing telephones and selling them to Office Depot. Then they would sell them to the consumers. Sometimes, large companies repackage the products you sell to them into their own brands, or they give you packaging with their design on it for you to package it in. At grocery stores such as Wal-mart, you see the Great Value brand. Wal-mart does not have their own manufacturing plants to make all of these different types of precuts. They pay manufacturers to produce the products and put the Wal-mart label on them. The other type of sales is direct sales, which are sold directly to the consumer through mail order, Internet, or through a retail store of their own. An example of this would be purchasing Gateway computers through http://www.gateway.com. Most businesses that are begun will be direct sales - directly from us to the consumers. My son opened a vegetable stand this year. He thought through what he needed and how he was going to sell the product. We helped him purchase a cash drawer for his money, a table to place his vegetables on, an awning to keep cool, and then he went to work in the garden. Once he opened the stand, he still needed to get word out that he was selling fresh vegetables out of the garden. He chose word of mouth advertising and free samples to promote his produce.

6.  **Sales**. Anyone can sell...or can they? All sales representatives need to know your product, believe in

what they are selling, not shoot prices or delivery times off the cuff, and do whatever it takes to sell – especially if they are on commission. When training sales staff, teach them:

- Sell solutions, not the products
- Sell the benefits, not the features
- Build relationships with the people they hope to sell to.

When making sales, remember basic etiquette such as speaking directly to the person, not mumbling, being polite, looking in their eyes, watching the use of your hands, and not playing with your hair, nails, etc. When in a retail operation and approaching a customer, make sure you say "Hello, how may I help you?" or "Hello, welcome to _____", or something along those lines. Yes, teenagers can be professional! Wear attractive clothing, not things that expose body parts or are so tight that they will distract the customers. There is a proper dress code for operating a business. There are a wide variety of businesses out there, so match your dress code with your business. These rules could be part of the policies and procedures manual.

Always be prepared! If you are going to make phone calls, think about it and be familiar with what you will say before you make the call. Be prepared to handle any situation. You might answer the phone to an irate client -how will you deal with it? Will their voice raising cause you to raise yours? Speak clearly and concisely. If preparing for a sales presentation, review the materials. Have everything you need at your fingertips, and no digging around for things. If this is a potential new client, ask them about their industry, what their history is with the company, and what they specifically need. Let them talk first, and get to know them before trying to sell anything.

Whether operating a retail operation or not, make sure to ask for the sale at the close. You can do this by asking, "May I ring this up for you?" or "Would you like me to carry that to the cash register for you?" or "How do you see my services fitting into your budget?" Make sure all salespeople have proper training in sales, customer service and in dealing with problems. If in a service business, when at an appointment, be sure to greet the client and shake their hand with one firm shake. Also, do not go in with a handful of materials and be tossing it around just to get a hand free! Keep everything organized neatly. Generally, people like a little small talk before you get into the sales. Make sure that to ask them what they currently do, how they see that you can benefit them, etc. Show them that you are there to help them complete a task, not just sell a product or service.

Always follow-up! There are different ways to follow up: phone calls, thank you cards, discounts, sending letters, and emails. Even if you use cards or letters, still phone the client or potential client. It is always better to talk to them in person. Work on building personal rapport with clients. Ask repeat customers how they feel you are doing as a business, what they like, and what they would like to see changed. Always contact customers who are not returning and ask them why if you have their contact information. You could turn a sour episode into a wonderful return customer. Keep an updated database of customers so that you can send them newsletters, new product information, or let them know of big sales coming up. Keep your business in front of them throughout the year!

In the book <u>Surefire Strategies to Growing Your Home Based Business</u>, David Schaefer came up with a way to put business prospects on a scale that is easy to remember, which he calls **AIDA**. This will help to see where the potential clients are and what is needed to get them to the action stage:

- A – Attention – your idea has got their attention
- I – Interest – they know that sometime they will need you, but don't know when
- D – Desire – they feel you will solve their problem or satisfy a want
- A – Action – they are ready to buy

7. **Pricing**. You must have accurate pricing for the market in order to sell your product. There are many gimmicks out there that are used such as: "Buy One Get One Free", "Buy One Get One at Half Price", and deep discounts. I don't think these gimmicks are bad, although they *are* gimmicks. People need to understand that these are not always great deals! The actual percentage off for a "Buy One, Get One Half Off" item is only 25% off! Some companies sell ordinary items that are extraordinary. An example of this would be Ghirardelli or Starbucks. These companies charge a much higher price for a regular cup of coffee or chocolate. They can do this because they have an exceptional product with a high demand. This is basic economics. If you start a coffee company and try to sell a lower quality product at the same price, you won't sell very many cups of coffee. If you come up with an original product, you have reason to sell the product at

a higher price. In order to determine pricing, know what your competition is charging and what your profit margin is and needs to be. **Profit margin** is the difference between the cost of the product and the price you can sell it at.

There are several ways to develop a pricing strategy. **Direct costs** and **indirect costs** will have to be factored in. Do not get this confused with direct and indirect *sales*. The direct costs are things like production, wages and shipping. The indirect costs are a little harder to figure out, but they include administration costs, accounting fees, and the utilities (water, gas, electric). These are also called overhead. Another factor to look into is customer demand, also called basic economics or supply and demand. Check out what your product is worth in your customer's eyes (**comparative value**). What about the competition? You need to know who they are, what their prices are, how is your competitor perceived, what are the return policies, delivery policies and fees, what type of guarantees do they offer, and what brand names do they carry. The final thing to look at is **substitute pricing**. This is what product you will substitute if you sell out of yours. Or is it better to offer a rain check?

If you set your prices higher than everyone else, offer something to go with that such as better service. This is called **premium pricing**. If you undercut competitors' pricing, it does not mean that people will automatically come and buy from you. You still need to draw people in your doors and offer them great service. Service is key! If you meet the competition's pricing, you need to figure out some way of comparing your products and service to others in order to show people that it is better to shop with you!

The amount of the company's overhead also needs figured into pricing. To calculate overhead, consider things like shelf life of a product, cost of shipping and handling, what the anticipated taxes will be, cost of insurance, cost of packing supplies, budgeted advertising expenses, and the speculated salaries. If the business knows how much a product is going to cost, there are some key tips to find out what it should sell it for.

If a company's goal is to make a 35% profit margin, they would multiply the cost of the product by 1.539. If the product was purchased at $1.00, sell it for $1.54. Why would you not take $1.00 and multiply it by 35%? This will only give a profit margin of 26%! That is a huge difference if a business calculates all of their products this way. The way I calculated this profit margin was by taking $1.00 x 35% which totals $1.35.

I took $1.35 - $1.00 = $0.35 / $1.35 = 25.9%. Thus, a firm needs to be aware of the multiplier which it should use rather than the percentage. To figure out the multiplier, take the starting number (choose $1.00) and figure out what you want to work out. So, say they need to figure out 20%. Take $1.00 x 1.30 (guessing) = $1.30 - $1.00 = $0.30 / $1.30 = 23% - so that is pretty close. The actual number for the multiplier to use is 1.25, making a 20% profit margin!

*Questions To Keep You Thinking*

1.  What is the percentage off if the sale is 50% off plus and additional 15% off?

2.  Calculate out profit margins for 25%, 30%, 40%, 50%, 60%, 70%, and 80%. What multipliers are used? Show your work.

3.  Write 5 jingles that you know and what businesses they go with.

4.  Cut 5 sale ads out of the newspaper, attach them to paper, and tell what the gimmicks are.

5.  Write a brief paragraph about both a positive and a negative sales experience you have had while dealing with a business. Address how you would have handled the negative experience if you were in management.

*Chapter 6*

# Management

One of the tasks in management is to ensure that the customer is happy. The easiest way to accomplish that is to have a well trained staff. Try to get things right the first time! Obviously, we are all human and make mistakes, so don't be too harsh on your staff if they make an occasional error. In today's society, customer service is 'key' to your business. Be sure to follow-up with your customers. The old saying, "The customer is always right" is not always correct, but you do want to bend over backwards to make sure the customer is satisfied. If they are not, offer them a solution.

Another job as a manager is to make sure the staff is well trained and knowledgeable on the products or service being offered. They also must use telephone etiquette such as taking notes, speaking up, being clear and concise in their communication, and remembering "thank yous" for calling. Not only does staff need to be trained in telephone etiquette, but also in people skills. Staff should look customers in the eye when they are speaking with them, and give them 100% undivided attention. There is nothing more frustrating than when sales staff is talking to each other or on the telephone while they are also "helping" you.

It is a good idea to read up about management and business frequently in order to see what else is happening in the world of business. It is easy to get so bogged down in the day-to-day operations of your business that you do not see what else is going on. It is a very time consuming profession! If you want a 9–5 job, a management position or an entrepreneurship position might not be for you. Read the newspaper and trade association newsletters to see what other business are offering to customers, or what types of new businesses are starting. Listen to the radio, paying attention to the jingles and advertising of other businesses. Know the competition and what they are up to!

If your staff is in the business office, make sure they know how to file correctly. Some companies prefer to file paperwork from the front of the drawer, and others from the back. Does this really make that big of a difference? Yes, it does! If someone is trying to find a certain bill and they are all mixed in with each other, it could potentially take quite a while to locate.

Whether you are a one man show, or a 100 person organization, you are a manager. As a manager, show others what you expect. Do you want your employees to be there 15 minutes early or 15 minutes late? You are the example. Don't have the employees setting the bar for your organization - you need to do this. If an employee's behavior is not up to standard, pull them aside and calmly explain to them what you saw and what you would like to see. Let them give their view of the situation as well. Be sure to have a manual with policies and procedures for dealing with difficult situations, including and not limited to vacations, pay raises, and improper procedures. Treat each employee in the same way.

Remember what the Bible says about how to treat workers....

Leviticus 19:15; "Do not pervert justice; do not show partiality to the poor or favoritism to the great, but judge your neighbor fairly."

Deuteronomy 16:18-19; "Appoint judges and officials for each of your tribes in every town the LORD your God is giving you, and they shall judge the people fairly. 19 Do not pervert justice or show partiality. Do not accept a bribe, for a bribe blinds the eyes of the wise and twists the words of the righteous."

Proverbs 31:8-12; "Speak up for those who cannot speak for themselves, for the rights of all who are destitute. 9 Speak up and judge fairly; defend the rights of the poor and needy. 10 A wife of noble character who can find? She is worth far more than rubies. Her husband has full confidence in her and lacks nothing of value. 12 She brings him good, not harm, all the days of her life."

Exodus 20:16; "You shall not give false testimony against your neighbor."

Proverbs 25:15; "Through patience a ruler can be persuaded, and a gentle tongue can break a bone."

As you can see in these verses, we are commanded to treat others with fair, impartial judgment. We are not to place any person above another, no matter what their status or circumstances might be. We are not to lie, be harsh or show unfairness to anyone. As a Christian business person, make sure to treat others as Jesus would treat you, and as you would want others to treat you if the situation were to be reversed.

A manager needs to know when it is time to hire or fire employees - this could make or break a business. If there is too much work and you are not willing to hire help, you will run yourself ragged and may eventually become sick and not be able to do the jobs you were doing. On the other hand, hiring too many employees is not a good thing, either. It is a large expense to hire employees. Analyze the work loads and your financial position to see if this is going to be cost-effective.

Not everyone is good at organizing, but it is a crucial to a successful business. If you are not good at organizing, talk to employees or family members who are, or look into another business that could help you improve. I cannot say enough about getting your business organized right from the beginning. You will make changes as time goes on in how filing is done and how merchandise is stored, but always start off with a basic system already in place. It is easier to change something that is already orderly than turn chaos into organization. It is a great idea to get input from employees on things like organizational systems, what products sell well, where you could use improvements, etc. Keeping employees involved will help them feel like a part of the business. This is how to keep them happy and productive! Have an open door policy where they can come in and talk to you about things - don't make them feel like they are beneath you.

**Time management** seems to be a big conversation piece these days. Basically, what it means is to use your time wisely. The Bible talks about this on multiple occasions.

James 4: 13-15; "Come now, you who say, "Today or tomorrow we will go to such and such a town and spend a year there, doing business and making money." Yet you do not even know what tomorrow will bring. What is your life? For you are a mist that appears for a little while and then vanishes. Instead you ought to say, 'If the Lord wishes, we will live and do this or that.'"

Ecclesiastes 3:1; "There is a time for everything, and a season for every activity under heaven."

Proverbs 27: 1; "Do not boast about tomorrow, for you do not know what a day may bring forth."

Matthew 6:33-34; "But seek first His kingdom and His righteousness, and all these things will be given to you as well. 34 Therefore do not worry about tomorrow, for tomorrow will worry about itself. Each day has enough trouble of its own."

We are to be good stewards of our time, whether it be at home or at work. Just like everything, God has given us all 24 hours in a day and we choose to use them in certain manners. Have you ever heard someone say, "I don't have enough hours in the day!"? People who are good at time management will rarely say this. They know exactly how much time they have and how long it takes to do something. Learn to prioritize and not procrastinate. There will be a lot of responsibilities that come your way that must be prioritized. Make lists! There are some people who do not make lists because everything is "in their head" - the problem with this is that no one can help them (how do you get inside someone's head?)! Try starting now in making lists of things to do. Start with your homework, if you like! Do not order a list based on what you enjoy doing the most, but rather, what is top priority. Acquire some education on time management if this is a problem.

One thing that is very hard to do for a lot of people is to delegate. This is so crucial to managing anything. We all have gifts and talents given to us by God. We need to discern what they are, and also what our strengths and weaknesses are. **Delegation** involves knowing what is better for other people to do versus what is better for ourselves to do, and then assigning jobs based on those strengths and weaknesses. Sometimes, jobs we delegate are not done exactly how we would do them, but if they are done well leave it alone. There are times when you will have to show someone how to do the same task multiple times, but just keep it up and eventually he or she will get it! You will both learn from this experience!

Proverbs 25:14; "Like clouds and wind without rain is a man who boasts of gifts he does not give."

*Questions To Keep You Thinking*

1.  Make a list of ways that, in the next two weeks, you prioritize your time. Then do it! Do not inform your family about this, and see if they notice any changes. Then ask your family members the day before class how they would rate your work.

2.  Find 3 Bible references on Time Management, write out the passage, and explain why and how these passages talk about Time Management.

3.  Write down a role playing situation of a customer or employee conflict. This could be a well handled or poorly handled scenario. Tell us why you think it was handled properly or improperly, and how you think the best way to handle it would be.

4.  Practice your delegating this week!

5.  Read and contemplate I Corinthians 12.

Chapter 7

# Business Tests

## Are You Ready For A Business?
http://www.usgovinfo.about.com

1. Do you have self-confidence?
2. Can you talk to strangers?
3. Do you have a passion about something?
4. Do you see a need in the community for something? If so, what?
5. Can you talk to people you know about something and sell them on the idea?
6. Is the time right for your product/service?
7. Are the buying trends and economy on your side?
8. Are you a hard-worker?
9. Do you need others to get you motivated?
10. Are you willing to sacrifice personal interests?
11. Are you willing to sacrifice financial stability?
12. Are you willing to work 80 – 100 hour weeks?
13. Are you competitive?
14. Are you willing to have no dependable income?
15. Will you seek out help if you need it?
16. Can you write your thoughts and dreams out on paper?
17. Do you have a good imagination?
18. When you see things going downhill, what do you do to turn them around?
19. What is your personality type?
20. Will you go the extra mile to see your business succeed?

### What's Your EQ? (Entrepreneurial Quotient)

Common characteristics in areas such as family background, childhood experiences, core values, personalities, and more turn up time and time again in studies of entrepreneurs. Find out how you fit the mold by determining your Entrepreneurial Quotient.

The following test is no measure of your future success, but it may show you where you excel and where you need to improve to help make your business soar. Answer the following questions with a "yes" or "no" and total your score at the end.

1.  Did your parents immigrate to the United States?
2.  Were/are you a top student in school?
3.  Do you enjoy participating in group activities with school friends, such as clubs, sports teams, or double dates?
4.  Did you prefer to be alone as a youngster?
5.  Did you initiate enterprises at an early age, such as a lemonade stand, family newspaper, or greeting card sales?
6.  Were you a stubborn child?
7.  Were/are you cautious as a youngster?
8.  Were/are you daring or adventurous?
9.  Do the opinions of others matter a lot to you?
10. Would changing your daily routine be an important motivator for starting your own enterprise?
11. You might really enjoy work, but are you willing to work overnight?
12. Are you willing to work as long as it takes with little or no sleep to finish a job?

13. When you complete a project successfully, do you immediately start another?
14. Are you willing to commit your savings to start a business?
15. Would you also be willing to borrow from others?
16. If your business should fail, would you immediately work on starting another?
17. Or would you immediately start looking for a job with a regular paycheck?
18. Do you believe being an entrepreneur is risky?
19. Do you put your long- and short-term goals in writing?
20. Do you believe you have the ability to deal with cash in a professional manner?
21. Are you easily bored?
22. Are you an optimist?

How to score the results (per question)

1. If yes, score 1 point; if no, subtract 1. Significantly high numbers of entrepreneurs are children of first-generation Americans.
2. If yes, subtract four points; if no, add four. Successful entrepreneurs are not, as a rule, top achievers in school.
3. If yes, subtract one point; if no, add one. Entrepreneurs are generally not enthusiastic about participating in group activities in school.
4. If yes, add one point; if no, subtract one. Studies of entrepreneurs show that as youngsters, they often preferred to be alone.
5. If yes, add two points; if no, subtract two. Enterprise usually can be traced to an early age.
6. If yes, add one point; if no, subtract one. Stubbornness as a child seems to translate into determination to do things your own way – a hallmark of successful entrepreneurs.

7.  If yes, subtract four points; if no, add four. Caution may involve an unwillingness to take risks, a handicap for those embarking on previously uncharted territory.
8.  If yes, add four points.
9.  If yes, subtract one point; if no, add one. Entrepreneurs often have the faith to pursue different paths despite the opinions of others.
10. If yes, add two points; if no, subtract two. Being tired of daily routine will often precipitate an entrepreneur's decision to start an enterprise.
11. If yes, add two; if no, subtract six.
12. If yes, add four points.
13. If yes, add two points; if no, subtract two. Entrepreneurs generally enjoy their type of work so much, they move from one project to another – nonstop.
14. If yes, add two points; if no, subtract two. Successful entrepreneurs are willing to use their savings to finance a project.
15. If yes, add two points; if no, subtract two.
16. If yes, add four points; if no, subtract four.
17. If yes, subtract one point.
18. If yes, subtract two points; if no, add two.
19. If yes, add one point; if no, subtract one. Many entrepreneurs make a habit of putting their goals in writing.
20. If yes, add two points; if no, subtract two. Handling cash flow can be critical to entrepreneurial success.
21. If yes, add two points; if no, subtract two. Entrepreneurial personalities seem to be easily bored.
22. If yes, add two points; if no, subtract two. Optimism can fuel the drive to press for success in uncharted waters.

Compiling the results

1. A score of 35 or more: You have everything going for you. You have the potential to achieve spectacular success.
2. A score of 15 to 34: Your background, skills, and talents give you excellent chances for success in your own business. You should go far.
3. A score of zero to 14: You have a head start of ability and/or experience in running a business and should be successful in opening an enterprise of your own if you apply yourself and learn the skills to make it happen.
4. A score of -15 to -1: You might be able to make a go of it if you venture out on your own, but you would have to work extra hard to compensate for a lack of built-in advantages and skills that give other entrepreneurs a leg up in beginning their own business.

From: Start Your Own Business, Rieva Lesonsky, 2001.

*Chapter 8*

# Business References

### Gross Profit Margin Multiplier

| Percent Profit Margin | Multipler |
|---|---|
| 20% | 1.25 |
| 25% | 1.35 |
| 30% | 1.43 |
| 35% | 1.539 |
| 40% | 1.68 |
| 45% | 1.83 |
| 50% | 2.00 |
| 60% | 2.50 |
| 70% | 3.40 |
| 80% | 5.20 |

Example: If you know something costs $1.00 and you need to make a 60% profit margin on that item, you will sell it for $2.50. This will give you a profit of $1.50 or 60%!

## To Debit or Credit a Journal Entry?
*Bookkeeping Made Simple*

| | | |
|---|---|---|
| An increase in cash? | Debit | Credit |
| A decrease in inventory? | Debit | Credit |
| An increase in machinery? | Debit | Credit |
| The spending of cash? | Debit | Credit |
| Going into debt (increasing a liability)? | Debit | Credit |
| Paying a bill that is due? | Debit | Credit |
| Earning revenue from a sale? | Debit | Credit |
| Increasing owner's equity? | Debit | Credit |

| Category of the account | If the transaction increases the account enter | If the transaction decreases the acct. enter | The Normal Balance is |
|---|---|---|---|
| Asset | Debit | Credit | Debit |
| Liability | Credit | Debit | Credit |
| Owner's Equity | Credit | Debit | Credit |
| Revenue | Credit | Debit | Credit |
| Expenses | Debit | Credit | Debit |

## References

Totally Awesome Business Book for Kids, by Adriane Arthur & Berg Bochner

Beyond the Lemonade Stand - Starting Small to Make it Big, by Bill Rancic

A Smart Kid's Q & A Guide on Jobs for Kids, by Jeanne Kiefer

Better than A Lemonade Stand!  Small Business Ideas for Kids, by Daryl Bernstein

Common Sense Business, by Steve Gottry

Small Business for Dummies, by Eric Tyson & Jim Shell

The Small Business Start-up Kit, by Peri H. Pakroo, J.D.

What No One Ever Tells You about Marketing Your Own Business, by  Jan Norman

Mancuso's Small Business Basics, by Joseph Mancuso

Anatomy of a Business Plan, by  Linda Pinson

The Complete Book of Business Plans, by  Joseph Covello

The Successful Family Business, by  Scott E. Friedman

The Complete Small Business Source book, by Carl
Hausman & Wilbur Cross

Surefire Strategies for Growing your Home-Based Business,
by David Schaefer

Bookkeeping Made Simple, by David A. Flannery

Start Your Own Business, by  Rieva Lesonsky

Petsitting for Profit, by  Patti Moran

Business Plan Pro website, from http://www.bplans.com

Can Do Biz website, from
http://www.candobiz.com/entrepreneur-
characteristics.html

Disciple Making Ministry website, from http://   www.d-m-
m.org

Kid Business website, from
http://www.teachingkidsbusiness.com

Accounting website, from
http://www.accountingbasics.com

www.ingramcontent.com/pod-product-compliance
Lightning Source LLC
Chambersburg PA
CBHW060149200526
45165CB00023B/1420